PARENT'S GUIDE TO THE MCAS* FOR GRADE 4

SECOND EDITION

by Cynthia and Drew Johnson

372. 1262 JOHNSON

Simon & Schuster

New York · London · Singapore · Sydney · Toronto

*Massachusetts Comprehensive Assessment System

Kaplan Publishing
Published by Simon & Schuster
1230 Avenue of the Americas
New York, NY 10020
Copyright © 2001 by Anaxos Inc.

For bulk sales to schools, colleges, and universities, please contact Vice President of Special Sales, Simon & Schuster Special Markets, 1230 Avenue of the Americas, 9th floor, New York, NY 10020

Editor: Maureen McMahon

Page Designer: Gumption Designs

Cover Design: Cheung Tai

Manufactured in the United States of America

September 2001

10 9 8 7 6 5 4 3 2 1

Library of Congress Cataloging-in-Publication Data is available.

ISBN 0-7432-1406-4

CONTENTS

INTRODUCTION

Although several years have passed since you were nine years old, your fourth-grade experience and your child's are probably not very different. There are still spelling bees at school, dodgeball games at recess, and giggling fits during class in which students try to stop laughing, but just can't. These are all memories you can share with your child. However, the experience of spending weeks in intensive preparation for three different multisession standardized tests is one your child will have all on his or her own.

The tests in question are the Massachusetts Comprehensive Assessment System, also known as the MCAS. The fourth-grade exams, which roughly seventy–five thousand children take annually, are similar to the various MCAS exams given to all Massachusetts students in grades three through eight. In the fourth grade, students take separate MCAS exams in English Language Arts and Mathematics. There was also a Science & Technology MCAS, but starting in 2001 this test is no longer given to fourth graders. Instead, fifth-graders will now take a Science & Technology MCAS as well as a History & Social Science MCAS.

Both fourth–grade MCAS tests are a mixture of multiple-choice questions and questions with extended open-ended answers. The English Language Arts exam also contains an early session during which the students must write a composition, while the Mathematics MCAS has five short-answer questions along with its multiple-choice and extended open-response questions. Critics of the test complain that some IRS forms are easier to understand than this test format. While this may be true, if you and your child familiarize yourselves with the test structure, your child will not be confused or frustrated by the test format and will instead approach the exam with the confidence of a veteran accountant handling a 1040EZ form.

How the MCAS Tests Were Born

Even though these fourth-grade tests do not cover past events, a little history here will help put the tests in perspective. In 1993 the state of Massachusetts passed the Education Reform Act, a $5-billion law aimed at doubling the amount of money the state spent on education. Among

> "We have to shock the system into realizing that standards need to be raised. If you were the commissioner of education, you wouldn't want these [low-scoring] kids graduating from high school—it'd be a disservice."
>
> —David Driscoll, Massachusetts School Commissioner

34 percent of all Massachusetts fourth-graders received a passing grade on the Math exam, while only 20 percent received an acceptable grade on the English Language Arts MCAS (66 percent of all students landed in the "needs improvement" category in English). Since then, scores have improved somewhat, but not as greatly as educators had hoped. For example, on the 2000 Math exam the number of students receiving an acceptable grade increased to 40 percent, a six percent increase from 1998. In contrast, the 2000 scores for the English Language Arts MCAS are virtually identical with the 1998 results, although the number of students who received a failing grade did decrease by two percent (from fifteen to thirteen percent).

These poor scores made state headlines in 1998, and in the following years the debate over the MCAS has only increased. There were student and parent protests before the spring 2000 MCAS administration, and in 2001 there were 46 MCAS–related bills pending in the state legislature. Though the dust has yet to settle, one thing seems clear: low scores do not mean these tests will be made easier or eliminated. The emphasis on standardized testing at all levels is growing stronger, not weaker. With "accountability" the pervasive theme in national education, more and more states are setting academic standards and then rewarding or punishing schools depending on whether they achieve these standards.

What's at Stake?

With so much emphasis being placed on the MCAS, you'd think the fourth-graders who take it should be given the right to vote as a reward (at least in state elections). Quite a bit is at stake, for both the child and the school district. MCAS scores are reported for students, schools, and districts. School districts that do badly may fire superintendents, principals, or teachers, although no specific plan is yet in place to deal with low-scoring schools. As for the individual fourth-grader, each school district must decide whether students who fail the tests can be promoted to the fifth grade, so the fate of the thousands of students who might fail will be determined by geography.

Math *en Español*—and Other Special Cases

The current criteria for whether children can take these tests in another language are quite tricky. Since the rules are very complex, parents of limited-English-proficiency students should clarify their child's test-taking rights with their local school districts.

As for students with disabilities, the state of Massachusetts has the MCAS-Alt program, which is designed to permit all students, regardless of disability, to take some form of the MCAS by 2001. Once again, parents should clarify their child's test-taking rights with their local school district.

How You Can Help

Many of you are already aware of how important the fourth-grade tests are to your son or daughter, which is why you picked up this book. While your child's teacher is probably already doing some exam-related work in the classroom, nothing is better for your child than receiving personal tutoring from someone she trusts, namely, you. Inside this book are all the facts, tips, questions, activities, and advice you will need to help your child succeed on the fourth-grade MCAS tests. The *Parent's Guide to the MCAS for Grade 4* lets you know exactly what skills are being tested on these two exams, gives you test-taking strategies to make approaching these tests easier, and tells you exactly how to teach your child these skills and strategies. By analyzing and discussing the tests in detail, our goal is not only to provide you and your child with the basic knowledge she needs to excel on the tests, but to instill a sense of confidence through familiarity, since feeling confident and prepared for these long, involved exams is a key factor in how a student fares on the tests.

After reading this book, both you and your child should feel ready to take on the tests first, and then the fifth grade. While that feeling might not do you any good in your adult life, it will do wonders for your kid.

Chapter One
THE As, Bs, Cs, AND Ds OF GOOD TEST-TAKING

Understanding the MCAS Tests Is Half the Battle

Does the mere sight of a No. 2 pencil cause your child to break into a cold, trembling sweat? Are the words *multiple choice* or *essay* invariably followed by a thin, keening shriek or forlorn wail? If the answer to either of these questions is yes, then it's time you faced the facts: when it comes to taking standardized tests, your child is just like everyone else.

The vast majority of Americans experience some fear and nervousness before taking a big test. It is only natural that a nine-year-old would feel anxious when faced with a test that might cause him to have to take summer school or maybe even to be held back a grade. Sure, a few folks out there are perfectly calm when faced with exams, but they are all either hopelessly insane or currently making a living writing test-preparation materials.

Let your kid know that it is normal to

The Breakdown

English Language Arts (ELA) MCAS

The test consists of five different testing sessions, including two Long Composition sessions given earlier than the other MCAS tests.

In the Long Composition sessions, the students receive a writing prompt, fashion a rough draft (Session 1), take a short break, and then write an essay (Session 2). Only the final draft counts toward the score: it is worth 0–20 points.

The other three sessions contain reading passages, which are followed by 36 multiple-choice questions (four possible answer choices; worth 1 point each) and 4 open-ended questions (worth 0–4 points each).

Mathematics MCAS

Three different testing sessions.

29 multiple-choice questions (four possible answer choices; worth 1 point each).

5 short-answer questions (simple fill-in-the-blank answers; worth 1 point each).

5 open-ended questions (worth 0–4 points each).

be nervous about the unknown, but that the more he knows about the MCAS tests, the less nervous he will feel. All the information and all the techniques we will cover in this book will ease your child's nervousness and replace it with confidence by making that "unknown"—in this case, the exams—familiar and manageable. Test anxiety almost invariably leads to a lower test score, so it is important you work to boost your child's confidence about the exam. Just understanding the basic format of all these exams can be empowering, as the test changes from a scary hurdle that must be jumped and becomes simply "an untimed math test taken in three sessions, with multiple-choice and short-answer questions worth one point each interspersed with open-response questions worth zero to four points."

The importance of knowing what to expect was clearly illustrated in 1998 when so many fourth-graders faced—and failed—the MCAS tests. This was the year Massachusetts introduced the test, and seeing it for the first time, 15 percent of all students scored in the lowest level in English, while only 1 percent made the top grade. Most likely, the new, unknown format unnerved the young test-takers. It was not that Massachusetts fourth-graders do not know how to write an essay or an open response; rather, the test format was so unfamiliar to them that they had no idea what they were supposed to write, or when they were supposed to write it. When faced with an unexpected, open-ended question, even most adults can become unsure of themselves.

Learning about question types and little details, such as knowing how many geometry questions will appear on the Math MCAS, serves a dual purpose for the tests: it provides your child with useful information, and it takes away the fear-of-the-unknown aspect of the test. This principle is the foundation of successful test preparation:

Familiarity leads to confidence.

Think of the MCAS as that haunted house at the end of your street. At first, your child only knows the horror stories about the children who went inside never to be seen again. Your job as a parent is to guide your child through the exams during the day, showing how the scary noise coming from upstairs is caused by a rusty blind, and that beyond the usual dangers associated with an old house (loose floorboards, a rickety staircase), there is nothing about the place to worry about. If you can replace the anxiety and stress your child feels about the MCAS with a feeling of confidence, you will have done your child a great service.

THE END-OF-SENTENCE GAME

For a fun way to quiz your child about basic MCAS facts, try playing this game. For one evening (or longer), try to sneak in simple questions at the end of ordinary sentences, so that "Please pass the potatoes" becomes "Please pass the potatoes if you know how many multiple-choice questions there are in the Math exam." Your child has to answer as quickly as possible, and correctly as well. The game can be one-player, with your child working to get as many right in a row as possible, or it can be two-player, so that your child can say, "Dear parental unit, would you please read me a bedtime story and tell me how many different testing sessions make up the English exam?"

Why Cosmos N'Deti, Former Boston Marathon Winner, Would Probably Do Well on the MCAS

Elementary-Level Tests

Although Mr. N'Deti, a world-class marathon runner, has probably not had as much work with fractions as your child has recently, N'Deti is skilled in one crucial test-taking area: *pacing*. Knowing that he's going to run twenty-six miles, N'Deti picks a nice, consistent speed at which to run and keeps at that pace throughout the entire race. What he *doesn't* do, and what you should not allow your child to do, is spend too much time in any one area or run out of gas before the race is over.

All the MCAS tests are untimed (the testmakers have designed each session to take about one hour, on average), but that doesn't mean your child should spend four hours taking every session. Taking too much time can become as harmful as taking too little: frustration mounts, boredom and fatigue set in. Perseverance is a noble trait, but on a standardized test, spending half your time answering one multiple-choice question is tantamount to standardized-test suicide. Your child should stay focused on the task at hand and never get too flustered by any one question. One or two small breaks during each test is fine if your child feels her brain is getting strained. Tell her to put the pencil down, stretch out her hands and arms, take some deep breaths, and then pick up the pencil and finish the test. If your child comes to a question she does not understand, tell her to think of this guideline:

> ***Spend up to four minutes trying to figure out the question, then, using the techniques taught in this book, take an educated guess and move on.***

The MCAS tests do not require perfection. There are only two real scores: pass or fail. To pass, students need to get about two-thirds of the questions right, so it is never worth their while to spend fifty minutes on one question that's stumping them, only to be so mentally fatigued that they do poorly on the rest of the exam. Certainly, you don't want to encourage your child to do less than her best, but she must realize that no one question is so important that it is worth getting bogged down on and upset over. There are always some questions that just seem baffling. Throughout the rest of this book, we'll show you how to teach your kid how to make good guesses, keep her cool, and stay on pace when faced with a stumper.

In addition to telling your child not to get stuck on one question, you can also encourage the "two-pass" approach to test-taking. On the first pass through a test, your child should answer only those questions she can handle quickly and easily, skipping over any questions that leave her confused or require a lot of thought. Seeing a bunch of ovals filled in right away often gives students a quick boost of confidence. On the second pass, tell your child to go a little slower, use process of elimination (a technique we'll discuss in a moment) to cross out any incorrect choices, and then take a guess and move on. The two-pass system is helpful on all MCAS tests, since it allows your child to answer all the multiple-choice and short-answer questions before tackling the multiple-step, open-ended questions. This is not to say your child should concentrate on the 1-point questions while blowing off the 4-point questions. The point is that the open-answer questions are harder and definitely more involved, and you do not want your child getting sucked into one of these to the detriment of the rest of the exam. By saving them for last, your child can answer all the multiple-choice problems, mentally ratchet her brain into open-ended-question territory (meaning she understands that these questions will be more involved and take more time than the multiple-choice questions), and then tackle them.

This point is also important for the English MCAS. After reading a passage, tell your child to answer all the multiple-choice questions on the passage first, and then answer the open-ended questions. This shouldn't be too hard to do, since the open-ended questions are quite often the final questions on each passage. Still, it is important for your child to realize these two question types primarily test two different skills. The multiple-choice reading questions predominantly test your child's reading comprehension level, while the open-ended questions are more like mini-essays testing your child's writing ability. Your child should focus on one skill (and one question type), then switch to the other skill, not jump back and forth between the two.

To help illustrate the importance of pacing, here's a little "test-prep fable" you might share with your child:

KAPLAN'S TEST-PREP FABLES: THE TALE OF ISHMAEL THE SNAIL

Call him Ishmael the Snail. When all the fish signed up for the annual aquarium obstacle-course race, no one gave him much of a chance, but Ishmael was confident of his abilities. The starting gun sounded, and all the contestants took off. The goldfish Ahab took the lead, but she got caught up on a whale of an obstacle early on. She couldn't figure out how to get around it, and she never finished the race. The two Ya-Ya loaches were also very fast, but they made too many mistakes. They kept swimming under the hurdles instead of over them, and they skipped some obstacles completely, so they wound up being disqualified. The gourami started out at a good clip, but he fell fast asleep around the plastic plant and Ishmael passed him. Ishmael ran the entire course at a steady, constant pace, rarely making mistakes, and when the final results were tallied, Ishmael was the winner. As his reward, Ishmael was named king of the aquarium. He now lives in a plastic castle and rules the fish wisely and fairly.

Moral: A steady pace wins the race.

Edgar Allan P.O.E. for the MCAS

One of the biggest advantages in taking a multiple-choice test is that you don't always have to know the correct answer. Think about it: the answer is already there, staring you in the face. If you find all the incorrect answer choices and eliminate them, you will get the question right just the same. *Process of elimination*, known as P.O.E. in test-taker's lingo, is a technique that good test-takers use instinctively, but with practice anyone can learn it. It is especially helpful on the Massachusetts tests because there is no guessing penalty. You see, on some standardized tests, a fraction of a point is deducted from a student's final score for every question answered incorrectly. This is known as a guessing penalty, and it is meant to discourage random guessing. On the Massachusetts tests, no points are deducted. A wrong answer simply results in zero credit, not negative credit, so your child has nothing to lose and everything to gain by making good guesses on questions she is having trouble answering. And P.O.E. is the key to good guessing.

To demonstrate the effectiveness of this technique, see if your child can answer the following question:

1. How old are the authors of this book?
   - A. 4 years old
   - B. 29 years old
   - C. 35 years old
   - D. 126 years old

If this weren't a multiple-choice question, your child would have little to no chance of getting the question right. However, as it stands she should have narrowed down the choices to either B or C, giving her a fifty-fifty shot of guessing correctly. Since, as we mentioned, there is no penalty for guessing, she should then pick either B or C and move on to the next question.

Use process of elimination to cross out incorrect answer choices.

Perhaps the hardest part about using P.O.E. is knowing when to use it. In the above question, for example, how would you know that A and D were incorrect? You could say you used common sense, and that would be a valid answer. In many ways common sense translates to a basic understanding of what the question is asking, and therefore what the possible answers could be. Ask your child the question below, and help her use common sense to get a general idea of what the answer will be.

Thomas had $4.00, but he gave half of his money away to his friend Jeremy for a plastic bucket. Then Thomas gave away half of his remaining money to buy some gum. How much money does Thomas now have?

Before looking at the answer choices, ask your child the following questions.

Could Thomas now have more than $4.00?
Could Thomas have no money at all?
Could Thomas have $2.00?

The answer to all these questions is no. The last question is probably the toughest. But even if the question is confusing to your child, she could still look at the answer choices and eliminate some incorrect responses.

     A. $4.00
     B. $2.00
     C. $1.00
     D. $0.00

Why would answer choice A even be there? Test designers offer choices like A to catch the careless student. They know many students often glance at a question, feel unsure of how to work the problem, then just pick a number from the question that appears in the answer choices. Using the process of elimination—and thinking about what the question is really asking—can help your child avoid these mistakes.

P.O.E. can also be used on the fourth-grade English exam. The incorrect choices are generated the same way they are in the above question: words are taken from the reading passage and placed out of context as an answer choice. Students who remember seeing the words in the passage mistakenly pick them as an answer choice, never questioning whether the answer makes sense. Here's an adaptation of a recent fourth-grade reading question:

1.   Where did Farmer Ike keep his cows?
     A. in the barn
     B. in a fenced-in pasture
     C. at a fruit stand
     D. in his house

Which of these choices can be eliminated? Hopefully, your child will recognize C and D as unlikely correct answers. C is wrong because stacking cows into pyramids is much harder than stacking apples and oranges, and D is unlikely because no farmer likes to have dinner interrupted by a stampede crashing through the kitchen. Still, these were actual answer choices, because the words *fruit stand* and *house* appeared in the reading passage.

Both of the examples of P.O.E. have dealt with the multiple-choice questions, which comprise roughly two-thirds of the MCAS tests. While P.O.E. is not the best tool to use when writing an essay, it can be used for some open-ended questions. Although these open-ended questions are not as amenable to P.O.E. as multiple-choice questions, many problems on the MCAS are multistep questions requiring the student to do more than one piece of work. In fact, on some questions the steps are even marked A, B, C, and so forth, showing quite clearly each step needed along the way. On questions such as these, P.O.E. is an excellent tool to find the correct answer or at least do work that deserves partial credit.

For example:

Michael reached into his desk and brought out seven pens, all shown on the top of the next page.

| blue | gray | red | orange | yellow | black | green |

Michael used one of the pens to color on a map. Use the clues below to find out which color Michael used.

Clues

It has fewer than six letters, but more than three letters in its name.

It is *not* the first or the last pen.

It is not next to the red pen.

What color pen did Michael use?

Explain the steps you used to find your answer.

In essence, this question is nothing but a three-step P.O.E. question, although instead of using common sense to eliminate answers, you use the clues given to you. With the first clue, you can eliminate red, orange, and yellow. The second clue knocks out blue and green, and the third clue eliminates gray, leaving only black. Even if your child messes up one of the clues and ends up with the wrong final answer, by describing which colors he eliminated and why, he could earn half credit on the question.

Although P.O.E. has many uses, one place where it is not effective is on the short-response questions of the Math MCAS. The short-response format is specifically designed to prevent test-takers from using P.O.E. to find an answer. However, other methods to get the right answer will be discussed in the Math chapter.

Have an Answer for Everything

Suppose your child comes to a multiple-choice math question that she can't figure out at all. Should she leave this question blank and move on to the next question? The answer is "No, no, no, no, no, a thousand times no!" Again, there is no guessing penalty on the MCAS, so every question must be filled in, even if it means random guessing instead of educated guessing. Advise your child to:

1. Look for ways to work the problem using the appropriate skill. (On the open-ended questions, be sure to write down what skill you are applying, as discussion of the right technique could earn partial credit.)

2. Use P.O.E. to cross out incorrect answers.

3. Guess and move on, knowing that passing your test does not depend on every little question.

If your son or daughter needs further convincing about the benefits of guessing, you might try telling the following story:

KAPLAN'S TEST-PREP FABLES: THE STORY OF KRONHORST THE FUZZY CHIHUAHUA BUNNY

Early in his life Kronhorst was just like all the other bunnies. He enjoyed carrots, frolicking in a pasture, and hopping up and down to his heart's content. One day, though, the Bunny Master came to all the bunnies in the world and said, "Okay, it's time you all got ears." (This happened a long time ago, when all bunnies were earless.) The bunnies had several choices to pick from: "long and floppy," "really long and floppy," and "tastefully long and floppy," just to name a few. Every bunny made a choice except Kronhorst, who couldn't pick between "cute and floppy" and "trippily floppy."

Not making a choice was the worst thing that ever happened to Kronhorst because, from that point on, everyone he met always mistook him for a fuzzy Chihuahua. "Look at that way too hairy Chihuahua!" people would cry, at which point Kronhorst would have to explain that he was a bunny. People would then ask, "But where are your ears?" Needless to say, Kronhorst got pretty tired of these conversations, as well as the endless invitations to the Hair Club's Annual Dog Show . . . although later in life he did make a lot of money investing in the stock market.

Moral: Answer every question on the exam or people will confuse you for a fuzzy Chihuahua.

While this advice is crucial for the multiple-choice sections, it is no less important on the essays and open-ended questions. There might be some open-ended questions that will look to your child as if they came directly from the Question Institute of Neptune. If so, tell your child to write *Neptune* next to it and come back later. However, he must not write *Neptune* more than once on any one session. On all other questions, your child should make his best attempt and make sure to document his attempt well. Who knows? Your child's guess might be the correct solution, or it might display enough sound math principles to garner partial credit. This is true even on the short-response questions. Even though your child's chances of answering correctly are slim if he just guesses randomly, an educated guess has a better chance of being correct than no answer at all.

The Only Way to Avoid Mental Mistakes

Nothing is gained by trying to solve any of these problems in your head. While it is impressive if your child can multiply big numbers without using pencil and paper or can work out scientific experiments in his head, it's not required for the MCAS. In fact, it even works against his score. Get your child into the habit of writing down all his work on problems and jotting down the main idea of a reading passage as he goes through it. Kids can eliminate a slew of careless errors simply by writing down their work. For many children, writing things down helps them clarify the material. Writing down work during practice sessions also makes for a better learning experience: if your child is wrong on a question, at least you can go back and see what the problem was.

Write down your work whenever possible.

As stated throughout this chapter, writing down your work is crucial on the open-ended questions. To illustrate this, read the following math example and then see how Imperious Student A and Well-Behaved Student B responded.

> Jonathan had $5.00 at the start of the day. At noon, he gave half of his money to Gwendolyn, and at 3 P.M. he lost $0.50 in a vending machine.
>
> How much money did Jonathan have at the end of the day? Explain your answer.

The Number One and Only Child in the Class

Students are naturally leery of answering a question they do not feel they know the answer to and prefer to say nothing unless they are absolutely sure they are right. Teachers see this all the time in classrooms: children refuse to raise their hand and offer answers to questions because they are afraid of being embarrassed by a wrong answer. Unfortunately, this habit will hurt your son's or daughter's test score. So explain to your child that, on these exams, she should act as if she were the only student in her favorite teacher's class, and if she does not answer, the teacher has to just stand there until she does.

Imperious Student A:
Jonathan had two bucks *because I say he did. Now all must bow to the brilliance of Student A!*

Well-Behaved Student B:
Starting out with five, Jonathan gave half, or $2.50 away, so he only had three dollars left. Then he lost 50 cents, so $3.00 - $0.50 = $2.50.

Not only is Student A a megalomaniac, he is also no better than Student B on this question. Student A provided the right answer with an inadequate solution, earning A only partial credit. Student B has the wrong answer but the right explanation, so B gets partial credit as well. Considering that about one third of a student's MCAS score is tied to the open-response questions, garnering a few points by properly showing your work could significantly boost your child's final score.

Although the example above is math-related, this technique is just as helpful on the English Language Arts test as it is on the Mathematics test. On the reading passages, have your child take whatever notes he is comfortable with, ranging from writing down the main idea to summarizing each paragraph. You don't want your child to spend a lot of time looking for the perfect phrase to describe the reading selection, but writing down any thoughts he has about the passage will help your child understand the passage better. Since many reading questions are testing just how well your child understands the action in the reading paragraph, any notes your child writes to aid his reading comprehension should lead to an improved score.

Writing down work is good advice for future MCAS tests as well. In the fifth grade, the open-ended Science & Technology questions often require a student to draw a chart or diagram. These questions sometimes ask a student to describe and/or chart a simple experiment, so writing everything down about the experiment is the key to answering the question correctly. Okay, maybe not *everything,* but you want your child to be in the mind-set to write down everything that he thinks is relevant to the question in order to get a good score.

The Matrix Questions

Right now some of you are probably saying to yourself, "Yeah, I saw that movie *The Matrix;* I can answer questions about it." Sadly, matrix questions on the MCAS have nothing to do with Keanu Reeves. Instead, they are the name the Massachusetts Department of Education (MDOE) has given to all questions that are on the MCAS that do not count toward a student's grade. You see, there is not just one copy of the fourth-grade Math MCAS that every student takes. There are usually about twelve different forms of each test, but about 80 percent of each form will contain the same questions. These questions are called the common items, and they are the questions used to determine your child's score. All of the questions that appear only on one or two forms and do not count toward a child's score are known as matrix questions.

This means that about 20 percent of the questions your child will answer on each MCAS test will not count toward her final score. The

While the matrix questions don't count toward your child's score, or the score of the school or district, these questions are used to determine percentile rank in question-category subscores. When your child receives her score, a section of her results will show how well she did on a specific type of question, such as Number Sense questions on the Mathematics MCAS. A score of 67 percent means that she answered two out of every three Number Sense questions correctly, so she could have had a test with six Number Sense problems—five of them common items, one of them a matrix question—and answered four correctly.

matrix questions allow the MDOE to experiment with problems that could appear on future tests. So on one hand, the matrix questions are helpful to future test-takers because they allow the MDOE to determine if the new questions are too hard or too easy, but on the other hand, your child will have to take the time to answer about seven questions per section that have no bearing on his or her test score. The presence of these questions reinforces that it is never wise to get hung up on any one question: your child might be spending all her brainpower to solve a question that doesn't even count toward her score. Tell your child never to get flustered by any one question.

"'Twas the Night before the Test . . ."

Make sure your child feels confident and well rested on the days of the tests. Hopefully, this means keeping the nightly routine as regular as possible. You might want to schedule some sort of activity for the nights during the tests, but it should *not* be cramming. Trying to jam in tons of information before a test is not conducive to a child's test-taking confidence, and it should be avoided.

A positive attitude is more important than any one fact.

If your child does want to review for a while, stick to the basics, asking questions about the test format and general test-taking strategies. These will come in handier than reviewing any particular parts of the Math and English tests. Also, your child will probably answer most of the general test-format questions correctly, which will boost her confidence. What you do not want is to have your child stumped by a series of questions, because then she will go into the exam the next day thinking she is going to do badly.

Here's a handy list of pointers for the time before an exam.

THINGS TO DO BEFORE THE EXAM

1. *Make sure your child gets adequate rest.*
2. *Give your child a healthy, adequate breakfast.*
3. *Let your child have medication only if she takes that medication regularly.*
4. *Participate in some activity at night that is fun for your child but not too taxing. (Watching a movie on the VCR or playing board games are two ideas.)*
5. *Give your child words of encouragement right before she goes to take the test.*

You get the main idea. Send your kid to school relaxed and positive, and don't do anything to upset her normal rhythm. Some things that would *definitely* upset her normal rhythm and should be avoided at all costs are:

THINGS NOT TO DO BEFORE THE EXAM

1. *Send her to bed earlier than usual, because she will just have to lie in bed thinking about the test.*
2. *Let your child have any noncritical medication (such as over-the-counter cold or allergy medicine) that will cause drowsiness or muddled thinking.*
3. *Unwind by watching the midnight triple-header of* Scream I, II, *and* III.
4. *On the morning of the test explain to your child how big the national debt really is, and what that will mean to her.*

Review

The Main Points

1. Understand the format of all the MCAS tests and be comfortable with them.

2. Maintain a consistent pace throughout the test, and don't let any single question get you flustered.

3. Use process of elimination whenever possible.

4. Answer every question.

5. Write down all work to avoid foolish mental mistakes and to garner possible partial credit.

6. Make sure your child is relaxed and positive on test day.

Questions to Ask Your Child

1. What's the moral of "Ishmael the Snail"? *A steady pace wins the race.*

2. Ask general questions about the test format until your child answers the queries easily. *How many multiple-choice questions on the English test? How many answer choices for every question?*

3. What does P.O.E. stand for? *Process of elimination.* Why would you want to use P.O.E.? *Because finding incorrect answers and crossing them out gives you a better chance of answering a question correctly.*

4. What's the moral of "Kronhorst the Fuzzy Chihuahua"? *Answer every question on the test or be mistaken for a Chihuahua with a hair problem.*

5. When should you solve questions in your head? *Never!*

6. Who will love you no matter how you do on these exams? *Your parents, of course!*

Chapter Two GRADE 4 ENGLISH LANGUAGE ARTS MCAS

The First MCAS Test: The Long Composition Essay

While the bulk of MCAS testing takes place in May, the Long Composition essay session actually takes places in late April. This test has two forty-five-minute sessions and consists of one essay question. In the first session, students are given a writing prompt and given paper to create whatever kind of rough draft they want to. (It could be a series of lists, a mind map, or just plain old notes.) After a short break between the two sessions, the students sit down and write out the final essay, which is then graded.

The system for grading is a little complicated. The essay is graded by teachers who assign it one score for Topic Development (0–6 points) and one score for its use of English Conventions (0–4 points). Therefore, each teacher gives an essay 0–10 points, and since there are two graders, the top score for a Long Composition is 20 points. To assign these grades, the teachers look at the following categories:

Topic Development (0–6 points awarded by each teacher)

Category	General Description
Idea Development	How well does the paper present and maintain a clear theme or idea?
Organization	Is there a coherent development of the essay, such as a beginning, middle, and end? Are transitional devices used properly? Is there a conclusion?
Details	What is the quality of the details used to support the main idea? Are the details credible and thorough?
Language/Style	Does the essay use the English language persuasively and eloquently?

English Conventions (0–4 points awarded by each teacher)

Category	General Description
Grammar and usage	Is the English language used correctly?
Structure	Is proper sentence structure used?
Mechanics	Are there any capitalization, punctuation, or spelling errors?

So if your child writes a brilliantly persuasive essay with absolutely awful English, he could get 12 points (6 points from each teacher for Topic development and no points for English Conventions). If he writes a totally unconvincing essay with perfect grammar, he would get 8 points. While it would be good to do well in both categories, tell your child:

Focus on writing the best essay you can, and worry more about grammar when you look over your paper at the end of the session.

Noah Webster to the Rescue

If your child is worried about his poor spelling, tell him to be sure to use the dictionary that is available during the Long Composition essay. Every classroom is required to have at least one dictionary for use by the students during this writing test.

Also, beginning in 2001 bilingual students will be allowed to use a word-to-word bilingual dictionary, but this dictionary must not have definitions. It must strictly be word-to-word. This dictionary may also be used on the MAth MCAS

Grammar mistakes can be found when your child looks over the essay at the end of the second session, while writing a poor essay to start with puts your child in a tougher position.

If your child is tired of studying different facts, equations, and other such information before every test, then the Long Composition test is going to be a breath of fresh air for him. Here is an important positive note about this essay:

All the facts your child needs to write the composition are already in his head.

No reading passages to refer back to, no short essays testing your child's understanding of a passage. Both of those things are waiting in the rest of the English MCAS, but Long Composition is testing one thing, pure and simple: What kind of an essay writer is your child?

To be more specific, the Massachusetts Department of Education wants to know what kind of narrative-essay writer your child is. On the day of the Long Composition test, your child will be given a narrative prompt that asks him to "produce a piece of narrative writing that chronicles and/or describes a particular event or experience." Here are some examples of narrative writing prompts:

1. Some vacations are better than others. Describe a vacation that was great for you and tell WHY it was great. Be sure to include details so the reader can enjoy the vacation as much as you did.

2. Everyone has done something interesting for the first time. Tell the story about a time when someone you know showed you how to do something for the first time. Or, tell a story about a time when you showed someone how to do something for the first time.

With roughly an hour and a half to write this essay, there is no need for your child to start wildly scribbling down the first idea that comes into his head. Rather, the key to the whole Long Composition test is in the first forty-five-minute session, when your child plans his response, outlining what he wants to say and what details he is going to use to back up his essay. And the more specific, the better. Look at the sample first sentences below, and see how each one gets more specific and, therefore, should lead to a clearer, better composition.

This is a story about how I built a car.

This is a story about how I built my first soapbox car.

This is a story about how I built my first soapbox car with the help of my dad.

I remember clearly the day I built my first soapbox car with my father's help: the morning was cold, chilly, as if the night were still battling the sun for possession of the earth, fighting to keep its spectral, frosty hands wrapped around our fragile planet.

These four examples could be graded Poor, Adequate, Good, and Very Good but a Little Melodramatic.

After thinking about and planning her essay, your child should spend most of the second session writing. Short, clear sentences are fine. Your child needs to vary sentence structure a bit, since graders are looking for that. But in general short, simple sentences are preferable to long, complex sentences because the longer a sentence is, the more likely it is to contain a grammatical or punctuation error—which could cost your child points. Remind your child that "stylistic brilliance" and "originality," though both components of excellent writing, are not among the criteria graders will use when reading her essay. She doesn't need to win a Pulitzer here. She just needs to stay focused on a specific topic and express herself clearly and correctly.

After she finishes writing, your child should use the remaining time—and hopefully she will have five or ten minutes if she stays on schedule—to check her work. One useful proofreading technique is rereading the essay silently but out loud; that is, moving your lips as if you were reading out loud, but not making any noise (since talking is not allowed). This slows students' reading speed down a little and helps them pick up on errors they might otherwise skim over.

If your child can plan, write, and proofread a tidy three-paragraph essay in twenty minutes, don't force her to use the writing schedule suggested above. There is no need for her to pad an adequate essay, and rambling on until time is up will just muddle the essay and increase the likelihood of spelling, punctuation, and grammatical errors. A speedy writer should use her extra time checking her work.

Sessions 3–5 of the English MCAS: Reading and Language Comprehension

The other three sessions of the English MCAS take place in May along with all the other MCAS tests. These three tests will contain about 36 multiple-choice questions and 4 open-ended questions that count toward your child's score. In addition, there will be about 12 multiple-choice and 2 open-response matrix questions that do not. There are three main formats that your child will see in these sessions.

1. *One passage, then questions.* This is the most common format, asking your child to read a passage of some sort (fiction, nonfiction; there are a variety of styles) and then answer multiple-choice questions about it, as well as maybe 1–2 open-ended questions. As we stated before, always make sure your child does the easier multiple-choice questions before tackling the more involved open-ended questions.

2. *Two passages, then questions.* This format is similar to the one above, with the students reading two passages and then answering multiple-choice questions about both of them. However, there is one key difference:

The open-ended question on the two-passage format will always ask the student to write about BOTH passages in relation to each other.

The open-ended question might ask your child to compare the lead characters in both passages or explain how they have similar themes. Your child needs to realize that the key to these short essays is to use information from both passages However, recent ELA MCAS tests have not featured the two-passage format as often as earlier ones, so there's a fair chance your child might not even see two consecutive passages (which are often short poems) followed by questions.

3. *Language usage passage.* Usually one of these passages appears on every test, and it usually consists of something like a dictionary page. Your child is then asked multiple-choice questions about words and their definitions on that page. To date, there has never been an open-ended question associated with these passages.

All three types of formats will be discussed within this chapter, but for now the concentration will be on the regular one-passage-then-questions format.

Many of the reading passages are culled from existing sources, such as *Cricket* and *Jack and Jill* magazines, which contain amusing, educational, and generally positive stories. If you want to give your child more practice at reading material similar to what will appear on the English MCAS test—thus lessening his fear of the unknown—then you should:

Go to a bookstore or library and start reading children's magazines with your child.

This will help on many levels. It will give your child more exposure to reading testlike passages, it should aid in his understanding of such passages (provided you help him with positive guidance), and it should improve your child's overall reading ability. And, as if that weren't enough, it's also quality time!

As for passage types, the selections tend more toward fiction than nonfiction, with folk tales being a popular genre. There is often at least one passage that looks unusual — it might be a letter, or a scene from a play — so have your child prepared for a wide variety of formats.

Most students are going to be most comfortable working on the multiple-choice questions, simply because reading a passage and then answering questions is probably something they have done before. Since answering the multiple-choice questions after reading each passage allows your child to work the easier problems first, this chapter will focus on the multiple-choice questions before discussing the open-ended problems.

Item Sets

The MDOE separates the questions that follow a passage into Small and Large Item sets. A Small Item set consists of 3-4 multiple-choice questions followed by 1 open-response (maybe), while a Large Item set consists of 6-8 multiple-choice questions followed by 1 open–response question. In general, the longer the passage, the greater the likelihood it will have a Large Item set of questions attached to it.

In general, multiple-choice questions after a reading passage fall into four major categories:

Word meanings

Supporting ideas

Summarization

Inferences and generalizations

Before we can start discussing each question type, we will need a reference passage, such as the one that follows.

Dashiell Learns a Lesson

There once was a young ant named Dashiell who loved to play all the time. Dashiell enjoyed spending time playing with his friends more than anything else in the world.

It was fall, and time for all the ants in the meadow to trek to their winter anthill in the forest. Most of the ants were busy moving their possessions, because they did not want to get caught in the meadow when the cold weather and snow came. Dashiell started to move some of his items, but then the weather was so nice that Dashiell decided to take a break and enjoy the sun for a while.

"Boing, boing" sounded through the meadow. Dashiell watched as Rebecca Rabbit hopped up next to him.

"Where are you going?" asked Dashiell.

"I'm enjoying the day by hopping back and forth across the meadow. It's very fun, would you like to join me?" asked Rebecca.

"Hopping seems like a lot of fun," thought Dashiell. He raised up on his hind legs and tried jumping like Rebecca did, but soon fell over on his face. When he looked up, he saw Aunt Dawn had walked up beside him.

"You still need to move your possessions to the winter anthill," said Aunt Dawn. "There's no better time than the present." Then Aunt Dawn crawled away toward the winter anthill.

Dashiell was about to go back to work, but then he saw Sylvester Snake pass nearby. "That looks like a fun way to travel," Dashiell thought. He lay on the ground and tried to slither like the snake did. He twisted his body on the ground for some time, but never made any progress. He stopped once his stomach started to get sore. Aunt Dawn saw Dashiell on her way back to her anthill and said, "All your belongings still need to be moved from the summer home. There's no better time than the present."

"Aunt Dawn is right, I should stop playing." Dashiell walked through the meadow. He heard the flutter of wings above his head. Dashiell looked up to see Carol Crow flying around in the air above him.

"What are you doing?" asked Dashiell.

"I'm flying around in search of food," replied Carol Crow, who snatched a tasty grasshopper out of the air.

"Flying seems like fun. Will you help me try to fly?" said Dashiell. He climbed up a nearby rock until he reached the top. Then he jumped off while waving his legs. Dashiell fell to the ground on his face. "Yipes," he cried, rubbing his head. Dashiell looked up and saw Aunt Dawn standing beside him.

"You still need to move all your belongings. There's no better time than the present." Aunt Dawn left to get more of her possessions and shook her head. "Will Dashiell ever figure it out?" she wondered.

As the sun set that day, Dashiell finally got tired of playing. "Time to get to work," he said. He went to the summer anthill and picked up some of his possessions. Just then a huge rainstorm broke out. Dashiell was unable to leave the summer anthill and had to spend the night in the cold, wet anthill all by himself.

The next morning at the winter anthill Aunt Dawn awoke and saw Dashiell crawling inside with a load of his clothing. "I thought you were going to play all day again," said Aunt Dawn.

Dashiell placed the pieces of clothing down and replied, "I need to move all my belongings here. There's no better time than the present."

Aunt Dawn laughed. "I'm glad you learned that lesson, Dashiell. Put that clothing away, and then let's go get more of your possessions to move to our winter anthill."

Dashiell Learned His Lesson: Now It's Your Turn

While reading through this passage, your child should be thinking about finding the main idea. What is the whole story about? The main idea helps shape the entire story, giving it meaning, which should hopefully help your child in his understanding. However, while learning the main idea is important, *memorizing* the main idea is not something your child needs to do. The passage is not going anywhere after your child reads it. It stays right there for easy reference. Teach your child to:

Read to understand, not to memorize.

Once your child understands the action of the story, then it's time to start answering the questions. Children sometimes try to read the story and then answer the questions without looking back into the passage for help. If your child does this, events could get jumbled together, and this will only lead to incorrect answers. Tell your child that the English MCAS test is just like an open-book test. The passage is there for her to reference, so teach her to feel comfortable going back to the passage to help her answer questions correctly.

Question Type 1: Word Meanings

Some words in the passage will have questions devoted to them, asking your child, "What does _____ mean?" It is then up to your child to figure out the meaning of the word by looking at the context, or how the word is used in the passage. Reading or hearing words in context is actually a good way for children to learn new vocabulary. It should be stressed that these are supposed to be new words, so your child should not be bothered if the word is foreign to him.

To help your child sharpen his ability to understand words in context, have him focus on the meaning of the entire sentence in which the word appears. Remember, on a multiple-choice test the answer is already there, so your child just needs a pretty good idea of what the word might mean in order to tell which answer choices are incorrect. Sometimes the meaning of the unknown word can be gleaned from the sentence it is in, but if the

Looking For Main ideas Everywhere

If your child is unclear on what finding the main idea means, ask him simply to tell you a story about something that happened to him at school today. Since almost every story should have a point, when your child finishes his story, ask him what was the most important thing about what he just said. Another way to phrase this is, "If you had to tell the point of the story in only one sentence, what would that sentence be?" The most important thing should be the main idea. Looking at a newspaper and discussing how headlines capture the main idea of a news story is another way to talk about the main idea. You can then read the story and come up with your own headlines. One exception: stay away from articles dealing with intricate, high-level finance unless you want your child's head to explode. By the way, if your child likes headlines, you can always play "Night of the Headlines!"—where one night everyone speaks only in catchy single sentences, such as "Child Heads for Bathroom!" or "Argument over TV Remote Leads to Conflict, Then Grounding."

meaning is not there, then either the sentence before or the sentence after will contain the necessary clues. Your child should never have to look any farther than that: this is a fourth-grade test, after all. As your child looks over these sentences, have him circle any clue words that help him understand the meaning of the word. In other words:

Read the words around the unknown word.

After he does this, he should be able to answer a question like the one below.

1. In the story, Dashiell thinks it would be fun to slither like Sylvester Snake. What does *slither* mean?

   A. slide

   B. fly

   C. hop

   D. crawl

THE MACKiNUTE GAME

A fun way to help your child learn about context is to play the Mackinute game. Take turns with your child substituting the word *Mackinute* into a regular sentence: the other player has to guess what the word *Mackinute* means in that sentence. For instance, you might say, "I like *my* hamburgers with pickles, lettuce, tomato, and plenty of Mackinute." If your child answers "ketchup" or "mustard" or some other likely answer, ask him to pick out the words that helped him or her figure out the definition of the word. Try to make the game as silly as possible. Good luck, and may the best person Mackinute.

Hopefully, your child chose answer A, "slide." As you can see, word-meaning questions do not ask students to give the exact dictionary definition of *slither*, just to choose the word or phrase that is synonymous with it. When you ask your kid which words led her to that answer, she should say the words "like the snake did" and the phrase "twisted his body on the ground."

If your child prefers, tell her to look over the questions before reading each passage and see if there are any word-meaning questions for that passage. If there are, your child should pay close attention to the unknown word in question when she reads the passage, in the hopes of understanding its meaning right away. This may help her feel more empowered about the test, but if it makes her lose track of the overall story line, it's not worth doing. In that case, just have her read the entire story, then be prepared to go back to where the word is in the passage.

Let's try another.

2. Dashiell raises up on his hind legs in the story. What does *hind* mean?

   A. rear

   B. above

   C. top

   D. front

The sentence with the word *hind* in it contains the clues "raised up on" and "fell over on his face," which might be enough for your child to figure out that *hind* must mean "back" or "rear." However, the sentence before also contains a clue, since Dashiell is discussing "hopping," an activity that every creature on the planet usually does with its back limbs, whatever they might be.

Question Type 2: Supporting Ideas

Plainly speaking, supporting-idea questions test how well students have read and understood small pieces of the passage. These questions are not about the "main idea." They are about the little details that, combined, make up the whole of the passage. For example, say you told your child the following story:

A clown in a blue suit walks into a bank with a large duck on his head. The clown goes up to a teller, who asks, "Is it hard to keep that thing balanced like that?"

"Not really," replied the duck. "I've got sticky webbed feet."

The supporting-idea questions would be things like "What color suit was the clown wearing?" or "What size was the duck?" These questions ask your child small facts about the passage that he is not likely to remember. If he tries to approach this reading test the way he takes most tests (i.e., by answering questions from memory), these supporting-idea queries are going to trip him up. Therefore, when looking at the English MCAS test booklet, it is important to keep in mind:

The answers for all supporting-idea questions are waiting for you in the passage.

Your child need not trust his memory on the English MCAS test. Remind him that this is an "open book" test, and using the passage is the best way to get these questions right. From memory, can either you or your child remember which is the first animal that Dashiell plays with? Even if you think you can, it is smart to refer back to the passage to answer this question:

3. Which is the first character that Dashiell plays with?

   A. Carol Crow

   B. Aunt Dawn

   C. Rebecca Rabbit

   D. Sylvester Snake

Looking back into the passage, your child should be able to pick C or eliminate A, B, and D, leaving C to pick. Either way, it's the correct response.

Here is another example:

4. Which character in the story says over and over
   again, "There's no better time than the present"?
   A. Carol Crow
   B. Aunt Dawn
   C. Rebecca Rabbit
   D. Dashiell

If your child decides not to look back at the passage, he might carelessly pick D. And he would be wrong! A review of the passage would lead him to the correct response, B.

Knowing where to look takes some understanding of the passage, but with practice your child should get better at reading a passage for its main idea while keeping a general idea of what events occurred when. Then answering supporting-idea questions becomes simply a matter of heading to a particular paragraph, reviewing the information, and answering correctly.

Question Type 3: Summarization
There will undoubtedly be questions throughout the multiple-choice section that ask, "Hey, what's the big idea?" More specifically, these questions want to know, "Hey, what's the main idea of this particular story?" Your child can learn to recognize these questions fairly easily, as the majority of them are written using phrases like "This story is mostly about ____," "What is this story mostly about?" and "What's the main idea of this story?"

Recognizing what kind of question is being asked is important, since the question type determines what strategies your child should use to answer it. In this case, knowing that a particular question is a summarization question is vital, since it means that the answer is *not* stated specifically in the passage. Your child could reread the passage forever and still not find the answer. That's why you should explain:

To answer the "mostly about" questions, get the Big Picture.

Your child will have to glean a general idea of what the reading section is about, then use process of elimination when reviewing the answer choices. Having a general idea of the meaning of the passage helps students pick the right answer, which is another reason why working with your child on finding the main idea is such a useful activity. The wrong choices are often actual facts from the passage, so they can be appealing options. But remind your child that just because a piece of information appears in the passage doesn't make it the *main* idea. A good way to think about it—and if your child can understand this, she's on her way to a successful career as a standardized-test taker—is that wrong answers on summarization questions are often the right answer on supporting-idea questions, and vice versa. Get it?

Think about the Dashiell passage, and what the point of the story was, then attempt the following question.

5. What is this story mostly about?

   A. Dashiell learned not to put work off until later if it could be done today.

   B. A rabbit, a snake, and a crow all played with Dashiell in the meadow.

   C. Dashiell carried his belongings from the summer anthill to the winter anthill.

   D. A crow flew nearby Dashiell, caught a grasshopper, and then flew away.

While B, C, and D are all factual, none of them encapsulates the main point of the story, which is A.

Question Type 4: Inferences and Generalizations

> ### HoW WATCHiNG TV CAN HELP iMPROVE YOUR SCORE
>
> Granted, there's a catch: it has to be educational television. But if your child enjoys watching nature shows, one way to practice summarization is to ask your child to summarize sections of these shows in her own words. Nature shows, on channels ranging from Discovery to PBS, are almost always broken down into segments, like "Here's how the meerkats defend their territory" or "Two rams fight to see who's the toughest ram in the herd" or "Here a pack of hyenas go to the automated teller machine to get some money for the baseball doubleheader." This game can be played with other shows, but nature shows are a good place to start, since the segments often have a general point, yet one that is never stated outright by the narrator, who is often spending all his time trying to sound majestic.

Inference questions, as you might expect, compel the student to infer an answer not stated specifically in the passage. Sometimes the question will have a phrase like "will most likely" in it, showing that the answer is not 100 percent definite. Like summarization questions, inference questions force the student to understand the passage and make deductions from it. For example, after the passage:

> Sheryl was sick, but her brother Tommy, who was in grade school, felt fine. Sheryl's three best friends in high school were Angela, Tammy, and Brenda. Brenda lived next door, while Angela and Tammy lived across town.

an inference question would be

   Since Sheryl is sick, who will probably take her homework to school for her?

   A. Tommy

   B. Angela

   C. Tammy

   D. Brenda

While this example may seem a little arbitrary (what if Tommy's grade school was next door to Sheryl's high school? What if Brenda went to a private school?), the question does contains the phrase "will probably," which goes to show you that MDOE (Massachusetts Department of Education) knows the meaning of CYA.

From the Dashiell passage, an inference question might look like

6. In the passage, Aunt Dawn kept telling Dashiell "there's no better time than the present" over and over again because she—

   A. wanted him to forget his chores and play all the time

   B. wanted him to stop delaying the important work he needed to do

   C. needed help moving her belongings

   D. is working for the top-secret government agency that is intent on helping aliens colonize Earth and that can only be stopped by two hardworking FBI agents

Nowhere does the passage explicitly state Aunt Dawn's reason for constantly telling Dashiell, "There's no better time than the present." It is up to your child to deduce from the passage that Aunt Dawn tells Dashiell that because she "wanted him to stop delaying the important work he needed to do," answer B.

Process of elimination can also be used on the above question, and not just on answer choice D, the "X-Files trap," which commonly causes Massachusetts residents named Mulder and Scully to perform poorly on this section. It is important for your child to realize that these passages are written at the fourth-grade level, and when it comes to emotions:

Good feelings beat bad feelings most of the time.

The reading passages are not written by a bitter, impoverished author angry at the world, no matter what anyone else tells you. They are written by former educators, and because of this there are no depressing stories about gambling addiction or people fighting and dying in a senseless war. So if you have an inference question asking how a teacher feels, you can always cross out answer choices like "angry," "hateful," or "moronic," and if you have a

What Kind of Question Is *That*?

Knowing the differences between the four question types helps you figure out how to approach each question. To work with your child and help him distinguish all types, discuss the difference between Objectives 1 and 2, which require specific information from the passage, and Objectives 3 and 4, which require your child to interpret information from the passage.

question about why an Aunt Dawn is acting a certain way toward her nephew, you can bet that the reasons are going to be positive ones. Aunt Dawn, then, is not going to believe choice A, which is negative, or at least not very nurturing of her. The best answer choice is B, as it is just the sort of positive, character-building answer that former educators writing the test would want children to learn.

Explaining the Open-Ended Questions

The most critical change between multiple-choice questions and open-ended questions is the one your child is least likely to notice, and that concerns what is being tested. Multiple-choice questions test to see how well your child understands a passage, while the open-ended questions test how well your child can write down her thoughts about what she has just read. Both are still tied to the passage, but the added component of writing an answer down in your own words makes it a whole different ball game.

Make sure your child is comfortable with taking off her multiple-choice hat and replacing it with her writing cap on each passage, because putting down a lot of words is one of the keys to performing well on these questions. This is not to say that writing down just anything is effective—your child cannot filibuster her way to a higher score. Instead, being prepared to write down a lot is important because being afraid to write *anything* is a certain recipe for disaster.

Since your child must back up the answer with information derived from the passage, make sure she knows:

If you can support your answer with examples from the story, then it is right.

Your child's answer might not be sufficient enough to earn the maximum number of points for that question, but if she uses the information from the passage in at least a fairly accurate manner, then she should garner at least partial credit.

Here are two sample open-ended questions on the Dashiell passage:

> What might have happened to Dashiell if he continued to play and never moved to the winter anthill? Give two examples from the story to explain your answer.

> What are some of the things Dashiell does to delay the work he needs to do? Use THREE specific examples from the story to explain your answer.

As for the first question, your child will have to understand the passage well enough to make some deductions about it. In other words, if your son thought that Dashiell would do just fine playacting like a rabbit for the rest of his life, he would probably not gain any credit on this question. However, if your son understands that acting like a rabbit for a long time is not going to help Dashiell at all, then he needs only to write that down and then back it up with a fact or two from the story, such as "If Dashiell keeps playing with the rabbits and snakes, he will have to stay at the summer anthill, which is cold and wet."

At first, your child may be resistant to the open-ended questions, since most children prefer to know exactly the right answer instead of just jotting down whatever thoughts they have. However, it is crucial to your child's success on these open-ended questions that he feel comfortable in putting down his thoughts on paper. If your child is not so thrilled about writing down his thoughts, here's a story to boost his confidence.

KAPLAN'S TEST-PREP FABLES: THE PRINCESS WHO WANTED TWO BADGERS AND CEMENT BOOTS

Everyone agreed, Princess Lori was without doubt the most beautiful and difficult person in the entire kingdom. When the king asked whose hand she wanted in marriage, Lori replied she would take the first man who came through the front castle door wearing cement boots and carrying a badger in each hand. From anyone else, this statement would have been called ridiculous, but coming from Lori, it was not even the fourth most difficult request she made that day.

Lured by her beauty, many suitors tried, but all failed. These men learned the hard way that knocking on a door or turning a handle when carrying a badger is an almost impossible task, especially if you have sensitive fingers. And these men were better than most, who got shinsplints from wearing cement shoes and never even made it out of the construction area.

But one day Umbagog the Woodsman came to the castle. A fierce man, Umbagog was so tough he normally cut down trees just by staring at them until they fell over in fright. Umbagog showed up outside the castle wearing cement shoes with steel-girder laces while holding two of the biggest, meanest badgers anyone had ever seen. He took one look at the door, then slammed his head against it, shattering it in one blow. Umbagog then married Princess Lori, and they both lived happily ever after for reasons no one could ever quite explain.

Moral: In tough situations, don't be afraid to use your head.

Another general point your child must remember is that pacing continues to be important while answering open-ended questions. It is easy to lose track of time when writing an essay. You start worrying over exactly how to phrase something, and pretty soon the test is already half over, and you have only read one passage. Granted, the MCAS is untimed, but you don't want your child using all her brainpower on only one passage. Instead, tell her to:

Set a pace and watch your watch.

Of course, this means you will need to give your child a watch to wear (or make sure there is a clock in her classroom) and be certain she knows how to read it. Refer to the following chart for pacing suggestions:

Question	Time Spent
Reading the passage	5–7 minutes per passage
Multiple-choice questions	1–2 minutes per question
Open-ended questions	5–10 minutes per question

Once again, though, the key is not to spend too much time on any one question at the expense of the entire test.

The Two-Passages-then-Questions Format

Sometimes the two passages will be quite short, like two poems. However, that is not always the case, and your child might have to read two long, seven-hundred-word passages before ever seeing a question. This can be frustrating, as your child is spending all the time reading and no time answering questions, which is the whole point of the MCAS. If you like, then, tell your child:

> *If you come across two passages in a row, read the first one, then answer all the multiple-choice questions about it. Then read the second passage and do the same.*

This is a useful suggestion since it allows your child to tackle the relevant multiple-choice questions while each passage is still fresh in her head. In general, the multiple-choice questions related to the first passage come first and are followed by multiple-choice questions for the second passage, so there's little chance of your child attempting to answer a question on the passage she has not yet read. The questions themselves often refer specifically to a passage.

To gain full credit on open-ended questions combining two passages, your child needs to remember two main things:

> *1. Use information from BOTH reading passages.*
>
> *2. Make some conclusions and support them with details.*

DICTIONARY SPRINTS

This game requires one dictionary per person. Each person starts with his dictionary closed, and one player begins by making a statement like "First person to find an adverb wins." Each player then flips open his dictionary and scans the pages until he finds an entry with *adv.*, which is how a word that is an adverb is usually designated. The winner gets a point. Other sprints could include "first person to find a word with a Latin root" or "first person to find a word with six or more definitions"—we recommend looking up the word *set*—or even "first person to find an entry with a synonym." Since you need to understand a dictionary to play the game, teach your child along the way or turn to the front of the dictionary to learn about all the different terminology.

She cannot just talk about one passage at the expense of the other one. Except for combining information from two passages in the best possible manner, these open-ended questions are like any others.

Language Usage Passage

These passages come in two main forms: the dictionary page and a Root Box, which is a collection of English word roots and prefixes. On the dictionary multiple-choice questions, questions center around such things as:

What is the original meaning of a word?

What is its part of speech? (noun, verb, adjective, and so forth)

How is it pluralized?

What are some synonyms or antonyms of the word?

All these questions basically test how well your child can use a dictionary, so the simplest way to prepare for these questions is to:

Make sure your child can use a dictionary.

The Root Box problems look freaky, but they really just boil down to a game of matching. A typical Root Box would look like:

```
trans = across

bio = life

psych = mind

logy = science

continent = body of land

mass = body of matter
```

with questions such as:

1. What word below means "to travel across a body of land"?

    A. transcontinental

    B. transmass

    C. biomass

    D. transology

2. The science, or study, of the mind is known as
    A. biology
    B. psychmass
    C. transology
    D. psychology

If the strangeness of the format does not disrupt your child's thinking, these questions are easily solved.

> *On the Root Box questions, go up to the Root Box and find the proper parts (they'll be on the left side of the equations), then stick them together. Some assembly is required.*

For the first question, your child takes the word "across" from the question and finds the prefix *trans*, which she then jams onto *continent*, since it means *body of land*. The answer is A. The same process is used for the next question, and your child should get D.

Chapter Three GRADE 4 MCAS MATHEMATICS

How the Math Test Adds Up

The Grade 4 MCAS Mathematics has three testing sessions and a variety of multiple-choice, short-answer, and open-response questions. The breakdown is as follows:

GRADE 4 MCAS MATH BREAKDOWN

29 multiple-choice questions worth 1 point each.

5 short-answer questions worth 1 point each
(these are like fill-in-the-blank math questions).

5 open-ended questions worth 0–4 points.

NOTE: The exam also includes roughly 7 multiple–choice, 1 short–answer, and 1 open–ended matrix questions.

Since this is a math exam, let's do some math and analyze the question type breakdown. Although the number of questions of each type might vary slightly one year to the next, in general the above numbers are reliable. A perfect score on this test would total 54 points.

In this scenario, taking a lot of time to get the 5 open-ended responses correct would mean you gain 20 points on those five problems. That sounds all well and good, except for the fact that the multiple choice and grid questions account for 63% of the entire test. The open-ended questions take a lot of time and, combined, account for only about one-third of a student's final grade. With this in mind, tell your child:

Take the time to answer all the multiple-choice and short-answer questions first, then use the time remaining to answer the open-ended problems.

If your child does not follow this advice, there are two major pitfalls he could find. He might set out to take the test from start to finish, but along the way get caught up working a long, difficult open-ended question and get bogged down and mentally fatigued. He blows his chance at correctly answering several less complicated multiple-choice questions worth more points by working that difficult open-ended question. He might also get in trouble if he rushes through the multiple-choice questions to have more time to answer the open-ended problems. This means your child has rushed through 63 percent of the potential test points to work on tough, involved problems that are not as important to his overall score. Both of the scenarios lead your child toward a lower grade, and they should be avoided at all costs.

Here is another advantage with using a two-pass system on the MCAS Math, answering all the multiple-choice questions first:

> **The fact that the multiple-choice questions count the most toward your score is good news because test-taking strategies are most effective against the multiple-choice format.**

What you want your child to understand is that almost half of all the math answers will be sitting in front of him, and all he has to do is pick out the correct answer or eliminate any incorrect answers and then take a guess. Granted, some of the 1-point questions are short-response questions, which are immune to P.O.E., but even so, multiple-choice questions outnumber the short-answer questions by a fair amount.

An Open-Ended Discussion about Open-Ended Questions

While the multiple-choice part of the exam is scored by a machine, the 4-point questions are scored primarily by Massachusetts educators who have been given guidelines about what constitutes a 4-point response, a 3-point response, a 2-point response, and so on. To get full credit your child has to respond in a manner that is "complete and correct," meaning that not only is the correct answer visible, but there is also adequate work shown that demonstrates your child arrived at the answer by using her math skills and not her powerful psychic ability.* If your child has the correct answer, but without any explanation, the response is not worth as much. So, as we stated in chapter 1, remind your child that on every open-ended question:

> **Show your work, and give every question your best shot using sound math skills.**

The following little fable might help convince your child of the importance of this strategy:

---

*If your child does have such psychic abilities, tell her to concentrate her mental efforts on the multiple-choice section, since you do not have to show any work on those questions.

KAPLAN'S TEST-PREP FABLES: THADDEUS THE ARTIST AND THE 51 PERCENT FIRING SQUAD

One day in the kingdom of Schmooland, the king's loyal attendants were dusting the king's favorite painting of himself when they made an unwelcome discovery. Some villainous knave had painted a tacky mustache and ridiculous horns on the royal portrait! The whole kingdom went into an uproar, and the king demanded that all subjects search for the person responsible. Eventually, many Schmoolandians started to whisper that Thaddeus the Artist was the person who had made the unflattering additions to the painting. These people had no evidence, but were jealous of Thaddeus and his hip, downtown lifestyle that included lots of coffee drinking, black turtlenecks, and incense.

In a rage, the king wanted justice, and although there was no real evidence, a judge declared Thaddeus guilty and ordered him executed.

"But, Judge," replied Thaddeus, "since there's no actual proof that I committed this crime, isn't it unfair to say that I'm one hundred percent guilty? Isn't it more like I'm fifty-one percent guilty, and forty-nine percent innocent?" The judge pondered this statement and, realizing that his judgment was only given because the king was angry, decided that Thaddeus was indeed only 51 percent guilty.

The day of the execution arrived, and Thaddeus was placed before the firing squad. When asked if he had a final request, Thaddeus said, "Since I am only fifty-one percent guilty, I should only be fifty-one percent executed." The officer in charge of the firing squad agreed and ordered his men to use only 51 percent of the usual gunpowder. When fired, the weakened bullets bounced off the artist's stiff smock, which was covered in dried paint and shellac. The officer in charge decided he had done his job, and let Thaddeus go.

A free man, Thaddeus found the real culprit, and then he wrote a screenplay about his exploits, which was made into a movie starring Harrison Ford that did tremendously well at the box office.

Moral #1: Partial credit can make a big difference.

Moral #2: Harrison Ford is a big-time box-office draw

All this talk about partial credit is not meant to encourage your child to not worry about getting the right answer. He should not answer the question "What is 7 minus 2?" with the response "Something around 3." The whole purpose of the discussion is to make sure your child does not freeze up when he encounters a difficult-looking open-ended question.

Free Stuff! Free Stuff!

If you consider the math exam as a journey, then the items the Massachusetts Department of Education (MDOE) gives to your child would be the provisions. Every Massachusetts fourth-grader taking this test is given a Tool Kit that contains a ruler, pattern blocks, and a paper clip.

The ruler measures both metric and standard lengths. There are fourteen counters and six different geometric shapes (a hexagon, rectangle, triangle, trapezoid, rhomboid, and square). The MDOE changes the exact contents of the Tool Kit from year to year, depending on the questions asked. However, it's safe to say your child will see something like the Tool Kit on page 51.

> ### MAKE ME A TRAIN!
>
> To give your child more experience with pattern blocks, cut out the shapes in this book and add a circle. Then ask your child to use the blocks and draw certain familiar shapes, such as a house or dog. You should start with simple shapes, then make the game harder as you go along. For instance, the first shape could be a car, but then the next shape is a fire engine, followed by a sports car, followed by a dune buggy. When your child can use these shapes to accurately draw a red 1964 Mustang convertible with an eight-cylinder engine, your work on this skill is done.

Whether your child decides to use the objects in the Tool Kit to answer questions depends on him. Tell him to think of the Tool Kit as yet another resource at his disposal. If he wants to use it, it will give him another way to find the right answer on some math questions.

Along with the Tool Kit, Limited English Proficiency students will again be allowed to use a bilingual word-to-word dictionary, provided there are no definitions.

What the Math Test Tests

The Grade 4 Math MCAS is designed to test Massachusetts students in five major skills areas of the state curriculum, known as the Massachusetts Mathematics Curriculum Framework. According to the Massachusetts Department of Education, these five standards are

Concept A: Number Sense   (Roughly 35% of test)

Basic math principles such as fractions, decimals, percents, number lines, estimating.

Concept B: Patterns, Relations, and Functions   (Roughly 20% of test)

Math concepts such as simple algebra (sometimes as a word problem), pattern questions, ratios, and variables.

Concept C: Geometry   (Roughly 12% of test)

Tests students' knowledge of geometric shapes, principles, and terminology.

Concept D: Measurement   (Roughly 12% of test)

Contains questions involving units of measurement (metric and standard), as well as perimeter, area, volume, time, and temperature.

Concept E: Statistics and Probability   (Roughly 20% of test)

Understanding and creating charts and graphs; probability questions.

The bulk of this chapter will cover these concepts in detail, but before we begin, we need to make one more point about the Grade 4 Math MCAS. In general, vaguely worded questions in this section cause students a good deal of confusion. Tasks in this section are rarely as straightforward as:

A New Concept

Recently the MDOE changed the number of major skill areas from four to five. This is not as shocking as it first sounds: a single category, Geometry and Measurement, was changed to two categories, Geometry and Measurement.

1.   Divide 48 by 6.

Instead, the questions are often trying to see not whether students can divide, but if they know *when* is the right time to divide. To accomplish this, the above question might appear as:

2.   There are 48 people who need to be seated at 6 different tables. Each table must have the same number of people seated there. How many people will be seated at each table?

Place your response here:

Or the same question might be seen as this:

3. There are 48 people who need to be seated at a restaurant. The restaurant has 6 different tables. Each table must have the same number of people seated there.

   a. How many people are seated at each table?

   b. In the space below, draw a diagram to represent this information.

   c. If the restaurant found two more tables in the storeroom and used them as well, how would this affect the number of people at each table?

   d. Two-thirds of all the guests leave by 10:00, and the remaining guests gather together. How many tables do the remaining guests need to use?

All three questions pose the same math problem, but to answer questions two and three correctly the student must be able to say to himself, "Hey, this is a *division* question." (The third question, as you may have noticed, was an open-ended question, while the second question was short-response.) This oblique approach to the key ideas is prevalent throughout the exam, which is why many intelligent kids get frustrated and wind up with a low score. They know a certain math skill, such as division, quite well, but they don't realize that the exam is often more concerned with discerning if the students know when they're supposed to use that particular math skill. Once your child gets comfortable with the MCAS approach to math, the math section gets a little easier.

THE CHANGE GAME

Number-sense questions also sometimes ask your child to read a word problem and decide what math needs to be used. If you do not mind parting with small amounts of money, one way to create word math problems is to play the Change Game with your child. Assemble a collection of pennies, nickels, dimes, and quarters, then present various amounts of change to her and ask her to tell you how many cents she has. If she gets the amount correct, add or subtract various pieces of currency, simulating addition or subtraction. Add or subtract the money in word form, though, asking your child questions like "If Bob has the amount of money below, and Bob and Joanie together have $1.35, then how much money does Joanie have?" You could also quiz her by saying, "If the amount of money here needed to be split three ways, how much would each person have?" You can expand the Change Game to include questions about basic number concepts such as fractions, percents, and ratios. If your child gets three answers in a row correct, she gets to "keep the change." If your child is very bright, stay away from using Susan B. Anthonys.

Concept A: Number Sense

These questions test a student's knowledge and understanding of such basic math principles as whole numbers, integers, even/odd numbers, decimals, fractions, ratios, percents (you know, all the basics you learned as a child but have long since forgotten). What makes these concepts difficult is how they are presented on the test. Consider this question:

1. The four students below are each wearing a T-shirt with a digit on it. What is the greatest possible number the students could make?

This is a question that covers up what it is asking fairly well. The trick is for your child not to get flustered if he does not initially understand what to do. He should ask himself, "What does this question want me to do with all these numbers?" After some calm thought, he will probably realize the answer is "Place the numbers in order from greatest to least." If your child is able to get over any initial weirdness associated with this question, she should arrive at 7,620 as her answer.

Make sure your child is comfortable with basic math terms.

Some of the more popular terms to know are *fractions, decimals, ratios,* and *percents.* Your child can be fairly certain there will be a question or two on each of these topics, so it is important that she truly understands and feels comfortable with these subjects.

The question above is a short-answer problem, in case you did not already figure that out. There will usually be one short-answer number problem that merely asks for your child to add, subtract, multiply, or divide correctly.

    2. 678

        x 83

Writing down all your work and avoiding careless errors will get you the right answer on the following question.

Number-sense questions also include two or three estimating problems. Estimating questions are general visual questions that ask students to eyeball a small amount and then decide how many of the small amounts will fit into a bigger amount.

2. This box has about 30 pennies in it.

   Which of these boxes has the amount closest to 60 pennies?

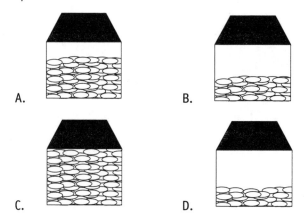

A.   B.

C.   D.

Note that on a question like this one, your child could use his ruler if he wanted to. It certainly could help your child estimate the height of 60 pennies, which should be twice times the height of 30 pennies. The answer is B.

Basic word problems also rear their heads as number-sense questions. To do well on word-problem questions, your child must take some time, perhaps even reread the question, then decide which mathematical operation is needed. Figuring out whether addition, subtraction, multiplication, or division is needed is a crucial part of all word problems.

Here is an involved number-sense word problem.

3. Prakash and his father were playing a game where one person would think of a number, and the other person would have to guess the number from certain clues. The first clue Prakash gave was, "I am thinking of a three-digit whole number that has the digits 2, 9, and 5."

a. List all the numbers that Prakash could be thinking of.

    Prakash's next clue was, "This number is also a multiple of 5."

b. List all the numbers that Prakash could be thinking of now.

    Prakash's last clue was, "When my number is rounded to the nearest hundred, it is 300."

c. What is Prakash's number?

d. Write three clues for another number game and number your clues. The game must have only one correct answer. Write the answer.

Quite a question, eh? All this for 4 points, which should show again why it's best to leave the open-ended questions to the end. Prakash's second clue, "This number is also a multiple of 5," basically asks your child to decide which of 259, 295, 529, 592, 925, and 952 can be divided by 5. Once again, it's a division question, of sorts, but it doesn't come right out and announce itself.

The correct answer for part c is 295.

As for part d of the question, your child would have to do a bit of work to gain that fourth and final point. Whether he cares to spend his time in this endeavor is entirely up to him, but the key point is, it should be done *last*.

THE LIBRARY GAME

This is an imaginative way to work on word-problem skills with your child. You start out with one book, and one person is the librarian, who adds to the collection, and the other person is Anti-Book Dude, who takes away from the collection. The librarian starts by saying "I purchased one book." Anti-Book Dude must now invent a way to take away two books, such as "Two books were destroyed in a small fire." The librarian must now add three books, but he cannot use the same way as before (purchasing), so he must come up with another way, like "Three books were donated by a wealthy woman." Now it's Anti-Book Dude's turn. Try to see how high a number you and your child can reach before running out of ideas. The early version deals with only addition and subtraction, but you can play the advanced version, which also uses multiplication and division, by posing problems such as "The library doubled its number of books. How many books are in the library now?" or "One-fourth of all books were eaten by locusts. How many books are left?" This game should help your child develop familiarity with the kinds of words that mean "take away" and the kinds of words that mean "add."

Concept B: Patterns, Relations, and Functions

Since this category makes up only 20 percent of the test, there won't be too many pattern/relation questions on the test, probably about five multiple-choice or short-answer questions along with two open-response questions. A simple pattern question will look like this:

4. Study the pattern below.

What is the next shape in the pattern?

A.

B.

C.

D.

On questions like these, tell your child to be prepared for patterns in groups of three or four, such as the problem above. Why these two numbers? While it would be rash to say that there will always be three or four shapes that repeat, consider what the test designers' thought process must have been. They probably thought a pattern involving groups of two would be too easy. Five is a remote possibility, but that would be difficult, so three or four are the prime suspects every time. Since it is a four-character pattern above, the answer is A.

> **On questions involving repeating patterns, first look for patterns that repeat after every three-four characters.**

Questions that ask you to add up the parts that make up the pattern are a little tougher, and they often look like the following problem.

5. This staircase is 4 steps high.

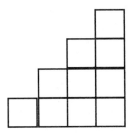

What would be the total number of squares if the staircase were 6 steps high?

A. 10

B. 15

C. 21

D. 24

To solve this type of pattern problem, *just continue the pattern and then add things up.* There are 10 squares to start with, so adding 5 squares and then 6 more would make 10 + 5 + 6 = 21. Then it's off to the answer choices! Our old friend process of elimination could help if your child got stumped on this pattern question. Clearly, if we started with 10 squares and then added more steps, choice A could not be correct. Your child can cross out this choice and then take a guess.

There are also some questions in this section that deal with basic algebra.

6. What number does q stand for in the equation below?

$(7 + 3) + 5 = 7 + (q + 5)$

A. 3

B. 5

C. 7

D. 12

Caution is the name of the game on this question. Your child can do the math, and so long as she writes down all her work and does not make a careless error, she should get the right answer. Or, she could look at the question and see that since only addition is involved, the numbers on both sides of the equation have to be the same. Since the right side of the equation is missing a 3, $q = 3$. Either way, the answer is A.

Concept C: Geometry

While measurement questions deal with geometric formulas concerning area, width, and so forth, geometry questions test students in several different categories.

Category	Example
1. Knowledge of different geometric shapes	How is a cylinder different from a cone?
2. Knowledge of geometric terms	What is symmetry? What is congruence?
3. Understand what an object will look like if moved	What will Figure X look like if flipped upside down?

To tackle the first type of geometry question:

Know all your basic two- and three-dimensional figures.

Two-Dimensional	Three-Dimensional
Triangle	Pyramid (with triangular or rectangular base)
Square	Cube
Circle	Sphere
Rectangle	Cylinder
	Cone

Knowing these figures is the critical first step to answering geometry questions well. Knowing these definitions backwards and forwards is even better, as sometimes there will be an open-ended question that will ask your child to give a definition along with her answer.

7. Which of the figures shown below is a quadrilateral?

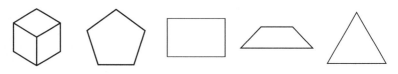

    a.   Draw a circle around any figure above that is a quadrilateral.

b. Explain what makes a shape a quadrilateral. Write your answer on the lines below.

_____

_____

_____

_____

c. A square is a special kind of quadrilateral. Explain what makes it different from other quadrilaterals.

This open-ended question is divided into three separate parts, and it illustrates how powerful partial credit can be. Even if your child makes a mistake and does not pick the correct figures (the third and fourth over from the left), he could still earn a point by answering the second part of the question correctly. Basically, any along the lines of "a quadrilateral is a figure with four sides" should garner a point on this problem.

In addition to shapes, geometry questions ask about such geometric terms as *congruence, symmetry, similarity,* and *reflections.* The test also has some questions concerning spatial sense. Students get a nice geometrical figure to start with, like

SUGAR CUBE CASTLE

For a time-intensive but fun way to teach your child about different geometric shapes, buy a box or two of sugar cubes, get some glue, and construct a small castle using the cubes. All the basic shapes can be created: the towers could be cylinders, the front wall a rectangle composed of cubes, and pyramids and triangles can be placed along the tower wall. To make a sphere, some careful nibbling will have to be done, but who doesn't like sugar?

and are then asked to pick this figure out of a lineup after it has been rotated in some way.

8. Which of the figures on the next page shows the top figure after it has been flipped both vertically and horizontally?

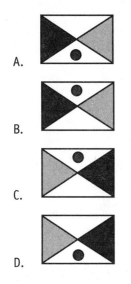

A.

B.

C.

D.

Two basic test-taking techniques come into play on a question like this. First, there is P.O.E., allowing your child to at least eliminate figure D, since it is the original figure. The second important strategy is "show your work." Do not have your child doing these mental flips in her head—have her draw the figure flipped horizontally, and have her flip the figure vertically. Artistic brilliance is not necessary, and neither is an ability to figure out this question in her head. Your child should just sketch out the two flips, which should not take too long. Even if it does take three minutes, three minutes spent getting a question right is better than spending two minutes getting a question wrong.

The correct answer is B.

Concept D: Measurement

Measurement questions, on the other hand, test your child's knowledge of such measurements as length, width, area, volume, time, temperature, and angles. In other words, does your child know how to find the perimeter as well as the area of a rectangle? And can she determine which questions ask her to find the perimeter, and which questions ask about area? The test booklet does not supply formulas for your child's reference, so she will need to be comfortable before taking the test with all the various area, perimeter, and volume formulas for the most basic shapes. She might encounter a question like this:

9. A group of construction workers stacked bricks in the shape below. Each brick measures 1 unit on each side. What is the volume in cubic units of this stack of bricks?

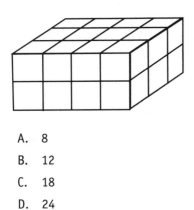

A. 8

B. 12

C. 18

D. 24

There are two solutions to this problem. The first requires your child to remember that volume = length x width x height, and so the numbers 4, 3, and 2 will need to be multiplied together to get 24. The other way would be for your child to look at the illustration and use common sense. Eight bricks are showing, but there are definitely more than eight, so answer choice A can be crossed out. At this point it is either guessing time or your child could now put together 8 x 3 (since it is three rows deep) and get 24.

Another kind of measurement problem tests whether your child understands the basic units of measurement and if she can use a ruler. Remember the Tool Kit? The question never says the student should use a ruler, but the short-answer question is tricky if you don't. And since no one uses metric units but everyone knows they should, you can expect that these problems will usually test metric terms.

On the short-answer section, there will sometimes be a measurement question asking you to use your ruler. Be prepared to measure in metric.

10. Jimmy the Wonder Slug, shown below, was recently found on a South Pacific island. The picture below shows the actual size of the slug. How many centimeters long is the slug "from teeth to tail"?

Place your response here:

Concept E: Statistics and Probability

The "statistics" part of Concept E consists of two types of questions involving graphs and charts: simple and advanced.

Simple = your child must read the graph correctly.

Advanced = your child must make the graph correctly.

As you might expect, the simple graph questions are usually multiple-choice/short-answer problems, while the advanced questions are 4-point open-ended questions. Simple graph problems may feature multiple questions referring to the same graph, and they look like this:

The following graph shows how many raffle tickets Ms. Diaz's class sold during one week. Study the graph, then answer the following questions.

> ### FOR THOSE OF YOU SCORING AT HOME . . .
>
> Various kinds of charts are scattered throughout every newspaper, but if you want to go to the place that charts call home, turn to the scoreboard page of the sports section. There you will always find as many charts as there were games last night. Explain to your child what the various markings mean, then ask questions like "Who had the most hits in this baseball game?" or "How many more runs did the Red Sox score in the fourth inning than the Yankees?" Questions like "This bum playing shortstop went hitless and yet still got paid $400,000 for the game. Where's the justice in that?" are socially relevant but should not be asked of your child because they rarely appear on the Grade 4 Math MCAS.

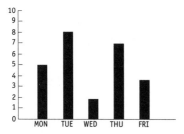

Ms. Diaz promised the class could work on their art project on the day the total number of tickets sold reached 16. The bar graph shows the number of tickets sold each day.

11. What day did Ms. Diaz let the class work on their art project?

  A. Friday

  B. Thursday

  C. Wednesday

  D. Tuesday

12. How many days did the students sell more than 6 tickets?
    - A. 2
    - B. 3
    - C. 4
    - D. 5

In both questions, the test never just asks for information from the chart, such as "How many tickets were sold on Tuesday?" In each case, your child needs to read the graph and then use the information in some manner. In the first question, this means adding up the ticket sales each day until the number 16 is reached, on Thursday. The second question is essentially a P.O.E. question: Which days can be eliminated because fewer than 6 tickets were sold? Only two days are left, leaving answer A.

An open-ended question might look like this:

Ms. Diaz's class sold raffle tickets for one week to pay for an upcoming class trip. The results are shown on the chart below.

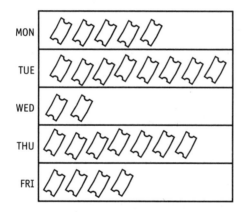

13. a. On a grid, make a bar graph showing the number of raffle tickets sold each day. Use the information on the table above to help you.

Be sure to:

- title the graph
- label the axes
- use appropriate and consistent scales
- graph all the data on the lines *provided*

b. Using the information from your graph, write
   two statements comparing ticket sales on
   the lines below.

At this point, no doubt many of you parents are feeling grateful that you do not have to take this test. Granted, this is a 4-point question, and deservedly so, but it can still be completed if your child feels good about making charts. Any number of answers to the second part could be correct. Graders want your child to show that he can interpret the graph he just created. A correct answer could be a statement like: "There are only 2 days where the students sold more than 6 tickets. The students reached 16 total tickets on Thursday."

CHART YOUR VEGETABLES!

To give your child some experience making charts, you first need to buy some grid paper. Then, it's just a quick trip into your kitchen, where you can ask your child to graph all sorts of items. How many vegetables are there? How many different types of soups are there? Make sure that your child always put numbers along the vertical line and a description of what is being graphed along the horizontal line. The rest is counting. If your child does a thorough job of graphing your food supplies, be sure to use the information on your next shopping trip. While everyone else has a shopping list, you will have a shopping grid.

In addition to charts and graphs, data-analysis and probability questions will have some questions dealing with the latter word, *probability*. These questions can come in many different forms, so there is not really any one particular question setup your child should be on the lookout for. Luckily, there will probably not be very many of these questions on the exam. Don't spend too much time trying to explain the concept to your child. You may frustrate and worry her unnecessarily. If she is curious, you can try using a die to explain the general principle. Show her that there are six total sides on the die, each with a different number of dots. The probability that any side will appear when you roll the die is one in six. That's the basic idea. It is probably best to leave the discussion at that, unless you want to confuse yourself and your kid.

Whew! Believe it or not, that's all the math. It may seem that there is a lot for your child to remember. There is. But practice using the activities suggested in this chapter (and any others you can think of), and she will be up to speed in no time.

Chapter Five I GOT A WHAT?!

How to Interpret Your Child's Test Scores

Your child's scores will be broken down into three main categories: a scaled score, an achievement level score, and percentage subscores.

The scaled score is a number between 200 and 280, with 280 being the highest score possible. These scaled scores are based on the number of questions a student answers correctly on each section.

Internet Information

For the most recent information about any of the MCAS tests, check out the Massachusetts Department of Education's Web site at www.doe.mass.edu. This site has a variety of information about the MCAS tests.

Every student's scaled score corresponds to one of the four achievement levels below.

Scaled Score	Achievement Level	Description
280–260	Advanced	Student exceeds performance standards
259–240	Proficient	Student meets performance standards
239–220	Needs Improvement	Student demonstrates only partial understanding
219–200	Failing	Student has serious academic deficiencies

The scaled scores are just a more precise breakdown of the achievement-level scores. In other words, since the minimum scaled score needed to receive a proficient rating is 240, a child who scores 250 and a child who scores a 255 will both receive this ranking, but the second child's test score was better than the first child's score. These scaled scores allow for a more precise ranking of schools and school districts, but as far as your child is concerned, the achievement-level score will be the most important one.

In addition to the scaled score and the achievement level, your child will also receive a percentage score in the English and Math content categories. The Math content categories are the ones discussed at length in chapters 3: number sense, measurement, and so forth. For the Grade 4 English MCAS, there are only three content categories: composition, literature, and language (the language subcategory deals with the dictionary and Root Box questions). The percentage subscores show how well your child performed on all those types of questions, so if she receives a 75 percent on the geometry-and-measurement subscore, that means she answered three-fourths of all those questions correctly. Note that the matrix questions are used when determining your child's subscores, but nowhere else.

While a low score can be a cause for concern, it should not necessarily be considered an indication that your child is lagging far behind in his studies and that his education so far has been worthless. Be sure to discuss his scores with the person who is knowledgeable about your child's ability as a student: his teacher. Your child's teacher will provide a better, more complete overview of your child's academic standing than a single numerical score from one standardized test. It is important that parents keep these scores in perspective. For instance, some parents might be disappointed if their child scores only at the proficient level instead of the advanced level. But in fact, only 19 percent of all Massachusetts fourth-grade students earned the *proficient* level on the 2000 English exam, and only 1 percent earned the *advanced*. Considering that about four-fifths of all students scored either *needs improvement* or *failing* on this test, any child getting a *proficient* on this MCAS fared well.

In terms of how the MCAS is scored, this is the end of the story. However, it should be noted that, in this case, the phrase "end of story" only means "end of discussion on how your child scored on one standardized test." Your child has about a decade of schooling ahead of her. This test should be seen for what it is: an interesting checkpoint along a very long highway. Some students who scored at the lowest level on this test will go on to graduate from prestigious universities with advanced degrees, while other students who scored at the top will struggle to finish high school. Your child's scores simply highlight where your child needs improvement. And the best person available to make sure your child receives that improvement is currently reading the last sentence of this book.

Ruler   Counters   Pattern Blocks

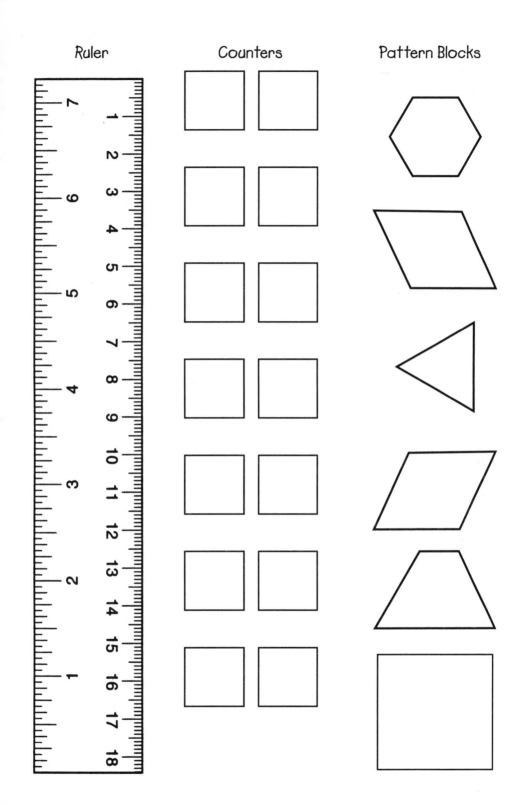

51